# PRAYERS & BLESSINGS

By
Carmel Carberry

Co-leader of Gardenland Ministries

**NEW WEBSITE FROM 2022
www.gardenlandministries.uk**

Copyright © 2016 Carmel Carberry. All rights reserved.
Produced by Amazon Digital Services 2016
(updated 2021)

Images by John & Carmel Carberry and Georgie Carberry (used with permission / all rights reserved)

Prayers and Bible readings are personalised and paraphrased within this book for ease of reading. Scripture references are offered in brackets for comparison and further study if the reader desires

*Special thanks to all our family,*
*and friends for your love and support*
*in so many ways. You are a continuing blessing*
*to us personally and to our ministry.*
*John & Carmel*

*Isaiah 58:11 says that The Lord will guide you always and that He will restore your strength. It also says He will make you to be like a well-watered garden and like a stream that never fails*

# CONTENTS

INTRODUCTION   Pages 1-3

PRAYERS inspired by The Psalms
Pages 4 to 14

PRAYERS inspired by Song of Songs
Pages 15 to 25

PRAYERS inspired by The New Testament
Pages 26 to 36

PRAYERS of Proclamation
Pages 37 to 47

PRAYERS of Praise and Thanksgiving
Pages 48 to 59
*Includes: 'Your inheritance in Christ' notes*

# BLESSINGS
## *Bible Readings to help in times of need*

*What does The Bible say about......?*

| | |
|---|---|
| ....*loneliness and isolation* | Page 61 |
| ....*fear and anxiety* | Page 64 |
| ....*depression and sadness* | Page 67 |
| ....*guidance and purpose* | Page 70 |
| ....*peace and reconciliation* | Page 73 |
| ....*forgiveness and guilt* | Page 76 |
| ....*failure and doubt* | Page 79 |
| ....*the truth of God's Word* | Page 82 |

**Encouragement from God's Son**    Page 86

About The Author and Gardenland    Page 87
*including social media links & more information*

# INTRODUCTION

In any relationship, communication plays a key role. When we talk with another person, we have an opportunity to share our thoughts and feelings with them ~ and listen to our friend's thoughts and feelings too. This communication promotes trust, friendship, love and appreciation in that relationship.

In the same way, when we talk with God, we deepen our relationship with Him. Prayer is basically communication with God ~ it helps us to develop our relationship with Him. And as we share our heart with Him we will find out that He wants to share His heart with us too!

This is because God wants us to ***know Him personally*** ~ not through a legalistic set of rules and regulations, but through a living relationship that is real today and for all eternity (John 15:15).

As I have grown in my own relationship with God, I have found that He can be trusted in *all* things ~ especially during times of need. As I have prayed (Rom 8:26-28) and cast burdens on Him (Ps 55:22), He somehow turns things into something good, in the final outcome (Jer 29:11).

Praying God's Word has been powerful in my own life, declaring what God says about me and my situation over and above my circumstances and/or feelings. Things in life constantly change, but God's Word is eternal (Ps 119:89).
For example, *Psalm 139:1-10* has been a powerful prayer as I spoke it out this way.......

> *Dear Father, Thank You that you know all about me and love me. You know my thoughts, see everything and are always with me. You place Your hand of blessing upon my head! You are great and too wonderful for me to ever fully understand! Thank You for being with me; You are My guide, strength and support every day! Amen*

In this book I have drawn from The Scriptures to produce some personal PRAYERS for individuals and/or groups to use, as they find helpful. My experience is that God has used encouraging words from The Bible to speak and remind me of His love. He is the same yesterday, today and forever (Jer 31:3 / Heb 13:8).

God is for you not against you (Rom 8:31) and He wants to encourage you! (Jer 33:3). With this in mind I have included a section called BLESSINGS to offer some brief Bible readings as reassurances of His love and grace always, especially during times of need (Heb 4:16).

After each selection of the personalised/paraphrased verses, there is page for the readers own personal notes and refection. God delights to shower you with blessings and He rejoices over you with singing! (Ez 34:26 / Zeph 3:17)

*Carmel Carberry*

# PRAYERS INSPIRED BY THE PSALMS

## PRAYER 1
### *Inspired by Psalm 121*

When I am in need, where can I find help that is trustworthy and certain? Thank You that I can always find help from You, The Creator of Heaven and Earth!

You alone watch over me both night and day
You are a cool and protective shade during blazing heat
You are my light and comfort during times of darkness

Thank You that for all eternity You will look after me
Thank You for being there each day of my life
And for staying beside me always!

~~~

**Listen to God's heart**
*"Do not fear, I AM with you at all times" (Isaiah 41:10)*

## PRAYER 2
*Inspired by Psalm 56*

Thank You Lord for Your love and mercy
When I am afraid I will trust in You
For You see my tears when I am oppressed

You hear me when I call to You for help
Your everlasting light is my guide ~ so I will not fear
For You are always there

Your Word is true and Your love for me is great
So I commit myself into Your loving care
Now and forever

~~~

**Listen to God's heart**
*"I AM for you, not against you" (Romans 8:31)*

## PRAYER 3
*Inspired by Psalm 75*

I praise You O God for how wonderful You are!
You hold my life together ~ even when circumstances
Appear to shake the world around me

You act with justice and yet You act with mercy ~ I praise
You because You are trustworthy ~ my heart rests in You
And my righteousness comes from You alone

You confront evil and deliver me because of Your
Eternal love and grace ~ for I am Your precious child
I put my faith in Jesus!

~~~

**Listen to God's heart....**
*"As you believe in Jesus, I lavish My love upon you, for you are My beloved child!" (John 1:12 / 1 John 3:1)*

## PRAYER 4
### *Inspired by Psalm 84*

Thank You for choosing to live within my heart ~ my soul
Delights in You Lord, and I am refreshed by Your
Presence within ~ I am greatly blessed in You

You are my strength always ~ even during difficult times
You turn my tears into pools of blessings! You hear my
Prayer and look upon me with grace and mercy

I always want to live in Your presence more than anything
For You are like a sun and shield to me
You never give bad things to me, for You are good!

~~~

**Listen to God's heart....**
*"Every good and perfect gift comes from My Heart ~ come
and receive good gifts! (James 1:17 / Matt 7:11)*

## PRAYER 5
### *Inspired by Psalm 91*

Thank You that I live in Your presence
Each and every day ~ I shelter under the
Shadow of Your Almighty Wings

You even command Your Heavenly Angels
To watch over me and surround me with
Everlasting faithfulness and perfect love

You are The Most High ~ my heart looks to You
Eternal King of Glory ~ I have made You my hope
And my refuge for all my days

~~~

**Listen to God's heart....**
*"I have loved you with an everlasting love" (Jer 31:3)*

## PRAYER 6
### *Inspired by Psalm 27*

You cause my light to shine and help me
Overcome fear ~ You are my stronghold and
Confidence whatever the situation

You are my delight and my place of safety
So I lift up my head and look to You Lord
Your beauty comforts my heart!

You never reject me, nor forsake me
You teach and guide me ~ Your goodness is
With me today and evermore

~~~

**Listen to God's heart....**
*"I will teach you and keep you in My Love. I will guide you and be with you always" (Ps 32:8 / Matt 28:20)*

## PRAYER 7
*Inspired by Psalm 98*

Lord, You give me a new song to sing!
There is no-one like You! You are wonderful,
Holy and righteous in all Your ways

You have given hope to the nations
And shown the way of salvation to all of mankind
Even the seas, mountains and rivers display Your glory!

The whole earth can shout for joy
For You are good, You are a righteous judge
And You show mercy to all creation

~~~

**Listen to God's heart....**
*"I have compassion on all I have made and I have poured out My love into your heart" (Ps 145:8-9 / Rom 5:5)*

## PRAYER 8
### *Inspired by Psalm 20*

God always answers me when I call upon Him
He sends help from His Holy Mountain
He is my support every day

He knows my name and
Watches over me from Heaven itself!
He even delights to give the desires of my heart

He is my success ~ He is my joy
I trust in Him alone! The power of His Name
Causes me to stand secure!

~~~

**Listen to God's heart....**
*"Delight in Me, for I delight in you! Commit your ways to Me ~ I will help you and make you shine!" (Ps 37:4-6)*

## PRAYER 9
### *Inspired by Psalm 103*

With my whole heart I praise You Lord!
You do marvellous things! You forgive and provide
Healing for me, even restoring my youth!

You are not quick to be angry, instead You are abounding
In love and compassion ~ You cast my sin far away
And show mercy to me

Your love is with ALL who look to You in awe and
Wonder! Your throne stands in heaven ~ Your kingdom is
Eternal ~ You make Your heart known across the earth

~~~

**Listen to God's heart....**
*"My Son came down from heaven to reveal My Heart ~ to show My love and mercy to all" (John 1:14-18)*

## PRAYER 10
### *Inspired by Psalm 139*

Thank You Lord for making me unique!
You know every part of me and love me totally!
You know my thoughts even before I speak!

Your hand of blessing is upon me and Your
Holy Spirit is within my heart ~ so I am never alone
Your Great Light drives away all darkness

You created me in a wonderful way
And my whole life is in Your perfect care
You are The Everlasting Way and I follow You

~~~

**Listen to God's heart....**
*Jesus said: "I AM The Way, The Truth and The Life" ~ follow Him and you follow Me (John 14:6 / John 10:30)*

# PRAYERS INSPIRED BY
# SONG OF SONGS

## PRAYER 11
### *Inspired by Song of Songs 1:1-17*

Thank You Lord, for covering me
With eternal love like a beautiful fragrance
You are My King who gives peace to my heart

I follow You because I love You
And You care for me like no other can!
You are beautiful to me and I am beautiful to You!

Your fragrance has become my own
You cause me to shine as You delight in me
I find rest for my heart in You

~~~

**Listen to God's heart....**
*"I refresh your soul, surround you with blessings, and give you My peace" (Jer 31:25 / Ez 34:26 / John 14:27)*

## PRAYER 12
*Inspired by Song of Songs 2:1-13*

Dear Lord, Your tenderness is amazing!
You care for me like a 'precious rose'
And provide space for me to grow in Your garden

You set a banner of love over me as protection
You support and provide for me ~ You embrace me
For You delight in me as Your beloved!

You tell me that 'the winter' of my life has passed
Therefore, I will arise to enjoy a new season
I have refreshed hope! And I am beautiful in You!

~~~

**Listen to God's heart....**
*"Arise and shine! Grow in My perfect love for you and rejoice in Me!" (Is 60:1 / 2 Peter 3:18 / Phil 4:4)*

## PRAYER 13
*Inspired by Song of Songs 2:14-17*

Thank You Lord for being my hiding place
A 'cleft in a rock' where I can find shelter
To calm a troubled mind by looking to You

I will not allow bad thoughts to spoil my garden heart
But instead I will listen to Your voice and be at peace
For You are mine and I am Yours!

You give me the strength I need to overcome
And as the darkness fades I see more clearly
That You have been with me all the time!

~~~

**Listen to God's heart....**
*"I never leave you and never abandon you; My love and guiding hand are with you always" (Heb 13:5 / Ps 32:8)*

## PRAYER 14

*Inspired by Song of Songs 3:1-16*

Dear Lord, my soul longs for You
And I seek You with all of my heart
For I love You with all that I am

Sometimes I feel that I may have lost You
Yet I find that You are still with me!
And with me all the time!

You have brought me out of the wilderness
Into a place of beauty and refreshment
And You rejoice over me with love

~~~

**Listen to God's heart....**
*"I continue to sing over you ~ I lead you to a fruitful place and support you" (Zeph 3:17 / Col 1: 10 / Ps 54:4)*

## PRAYER 15
*Inspired by Song of Songs 4:1-16*

Dear Lord, how wonderful You are
Your gracious eyes look upon with adoring love
And You call me to walk by Your side

You tell me that I am Your treasure
That I have captured Your heart!
You place a wellspring of life within me!

I will spread the fragrance of Your great love
In both the difficult and the good times
Whether the wind blows cold or warm around me

~~~

**Listen to God's heart....**
*"My Holy Spirit in you is an ever flowing stream of living water; to provide for you and flow out to others" (Is 58:11)*

## PRAYER 16
*Inspired by Song of Songs 5:1-10*

Thank You Lord for coming to me
And for making me Your own!
Your voice is comfort and strength to my inner being

You cause my heart to arise with hope
To begin to rejoice and sing
For You are my encouragement and joy

There is no one like You
You are awesome and outstanding!
You are the Lover of my soul!

~~~

**Listen to God's heart....**
*"I give you hope that does not disappoint ~ I AM your joy and peace as your put your trust in Me" (Rom 5:5+15:13)*

## PRAYER 17
### Inspired by Song of Songs 5:11-16

Lord, You are more precious than gold
And more beautiful than any precious stone
Nothing I desire compares with You!

Your powerful arms hold and comfort me
Your voice encourages and blesses me
Your feet produce footprints to guide my walk

You are my Best Friend and my Great King
You are closer than a brother and
The Greatest One of all!

~~~

**Listen to God's heart....**
*"I delight to call you My friend; come to Me in confidence, for I will always help you" (John 15:15 / Heb 4:16)*

## PRAYER 18
*Inspired by Song of Songs 6:1-13*

The eyes of The Lord see with perfect love
He looks upon me with amazing grace
And He sees the best in me!

My Lord has made me unique
And blessed me beyond measure!
He even rejoices over me!

His appearance is like the dawn
As fair as the moon yet as bright as the sun
And as majestic as the stars He set into place!

~~~

**Listen to God's heart....**
*"I created you like no other; I shine on you and rejoice over you with singing!" (Ps 139:14 / Mal 4:2 / Zeph 3:17)*

## PRAYER 19
### *Inspired by Song of Songs 7:1-13*

Thank You Lord that I am a child of The king!
Adorned with the love of God Himself
And crowned with His beauty!

I am the beloved of God
And my life is in honour of The King
For His glory and His alone

My life is like a fruitful garden
Where You love to dwell and take delight in
A precious place for You to grow good fruit!

~~~

**Listen to God's heart....**
*"I tend to My garden with love and grace; I plant good seed in you that grows abundant fruit" (John 15:1-9)*

## PRAYER 20
*Inspired by Song of Songs 8:1-13*

Lord, You refresh me and teach me
You have led me out of a wilderness
Into a place of blessing and peace

I lean upon You each day of my life
And wear Your 'ring' upon my heart
No storm can wash away my love for You

You build a wall of protection around me
You care for me and give me peace
So, thank You for calling my name

~~~

**Listen to God's heart....**
*"I lead you and watch over you like a Good Shepherd; and I have called you by name" (John 10:3+14 / Is 43:1)*

# PRAYERS INSPIRED BY THE NEW TESTAMENT

## PRAYER 21
*Inspired by Matthew 6:9-13*

I delight to call You my Father
And I bless and honour Your Name!
I pray for Your rule to extend across the earth
So that good is done here and in Heaven

Thank You for providing my daily needs
Your great love forgives me, so I also forgive others
Thank You for protecting me from all evil
And teaching me to walk in Your ways

~~~

**Listen to God's heart....**
*"My dear child, you are loved, accepted and forgiven through all Jesus has done ~ walk with Me and I will help you walk in love" (Eph 5:1-2 / 1 John 3:1-3 / 2 John 1:6)*

## PRAYER 22
*Inspired by Luke 1:46-55*

With my whole heart I worship You
For You are my Lord and Saviour!
You know my name and bless me
Because of Your mercy and love
And You reveal Yourself to all generations

You lift up those with humble hearts
And You continue to act in wonderful ways
You give freely to those who call upon You
You do not ignore the cries of those in need
And You fulfil all Your promises!

~~~

**Listen to God's heart....**
*"I hear Your prayer and delight to answer you! I provide help in times of need and fulfil all My promises to you"*
*(Rev 8:4 / Luke 11:9 / Heb 4:16 / 2 Cor 1:20-22)*

## PRAYER 23
*Inspired by John 17:1-18*

Father, thank You for the prayer of Jesus
I glorify Him with all my heart
Thank You for eternal life that He freely gives
As You sent Him to do in Your Name
So that all may know You as You truly are

When I look at Jesus I see You Wonderful Father!
I see Your heart in His words and deeds
He taught and shared Your Word
And let Your truth be known
So that the world could see and know You!

~~~

**Listen to God's heart....**
*"I sent Jesus to let My heart be known; to give new life, not to condemn the world but to save it" (John 3:16-17)*

## PRAYER 24
### *Inspired by Ephesians 1:1-10*

Thank You Lord for Your grace and peace
For You have blessed me in heavenly places
And shower me with blessings day by day!
You chose me in Your Son long before creation
And continue to help me become more like Him

In Him I am redeemed and lavished with love!
Your great wisdom is the revealing of Jesus
Who has set forth Your will for all mankind to see!
Your great plan is to bring all things together
United in Christ, in purpose and love!

~~~

**Listen to God's heart....**
*"I have called you into a New Covenant, of grace through My Son ~ I have blessed you so that you may also be a blessing to others" (Heb 9:15 / Rom 3:24 / Heb 13:16)*

## PRAYER 25
*Inspired by Ephesians 1:11-18*

Thank You Lord for my eternal inheritance:
Through Jesus I am included in Your family
And I am sealed by Your Holy Spirit
Who empowers me to live in faith, hope and love
Through knowing The Wisdom of Your Son

I will always give thanks to You, King of Glory!
I pray that the eyes of my heart may open to know
The depths of the hope to which You have called me
And to understand the wonderful richness
Of my identity and new life in Christ!

~~~

**Listen to God's heart....**
*"When you put faith in Jesus you become a new creation!
As My beloved child, the inheritance I give you no one can
snatch away!" (2 Cor 5:17 / John 1:12 / 1 Peter 1:3-4)*

## PRAYER 26
*Inspired by Ephesians 1:19-23*

Father God, how great is Your power
Which You have placed in all who believe!
How amazing that You have placed the same
Mighty power which raised Jesus from the dead
Inside of me! Because of my faith in Christ!

Jesus has The Name that is highest
Above all spiritual rule and authority
I delight in His Name and that He lives in me!
Therefore, I am powerful in Christ to do good
Because of His Life that dwells in me

~~~

**Listen to God's heart....**
*"I come to make My home in you the moment you receive Jesus ~ and I will always equip and bless you" (Rev 3:20 / Eph 4:12 / Heb 13:21 / John 1:16)*

## PRAYER 27
*Inspired by 1 Timothy 6:15-16*
*(also Jude 24-25)*

Our precious Father and King of Kings
You are blessed and high above all!
You are eternal and surrounded in Light
Majestic in beauty and honour
The One who rules over all creation!

In Your love and grace You keep me
And declare me blameless in Christ
Through ***all He has done*** for me
Jesus is My Saviour and Lord
I give Him all glory and honour due His Name!

~~~

***Listen to God's heart....***
*"You are redeemed in My Son; there is no condemnation and you stand secure" (Gal 3:13-14 / Rom 8:1 / Jude 1)*

## PRAYER 28
*Inspired by Philippians 4:4-9*

Dear Lord, I rejoice in You
For You are always close to me
And You are my help in every situation
Therefore, I will not be anxious about anything
But be thankful and put my trust in You

You are the protection for my heart and mind
So I'll think about You and all that is good
You are my Teacher, showing me Your ways
And teaching me to set my heart at peace
For You are with me, now and forever

~~~

**Listen to God's heart....**
*"I AM with you in all circumstances; look to Me and let My peace be your guide" (Col 1:17 / Heb 12:2 / Col 3:15)*

## PRAYER 29
*Inspired by Hebrews 13:20-21*

Father God, You are my peace
You who raised Jesus from the dead
And delighted in the New Covenant
That Christ willing and selflessly
Established in Your Name!

Thank You for equipping me
With every good thing
So that I may do Your will
And act in ways that please You
I give honour and glory to Jesus!

~~~

**Listen to God's heart....**
*"Every good and perfect gift comes from My hand ~ for I delight to do you good! I give everything you need and provide for you day after day (James 1:17 / Phil 4:19)*

## PRAYER 30
*Inspired by 1 Peter 1:3-5*
*(and 2 Corinthians 1:3-5)*

Thank You for Your mercy Lord
For giving me a new and living hope!
Jesus is alive and I live in Him!
My eternal inheritance is forever secure
For You guard it in heaven for me!

I bless You dear Father God and
Thank You for the comfort You give me!
How wonderful that I can also comfort others
With the same comfort You have given me
For in Christ, I am blessed!

~~~

**Listen to God's heart....**
*"Your love touches My heart; My joy lives within you so always rejoice, for your salvation is here" (1 Peter 1:8-9)*

# PRAYERS OF PROCLAMATION

## PRAYER 31
### Inspired by Romans 8:1-8

I proclaim Your victory Lord
And I will follow the ways of Your Spirit
For I am no longer under condemnation!

I proclaim the freedom Christ has given!
For He lives in me eternally and
He has overcome all things for me!

My mind considers God's Words
And I seek to please Him above all else
For His Spirit is life and peace to my soul

**Listen to God's heart....**
*"The Words I speak are Spirit and Life to you" (John 6:63)*

## PRAYER 32
*Inspired by Romans 8:9-17*

God's Holy Spirit lives in me
His fruit dwells within, therefore
I choose to follow His ways above my own

Jesus has made me right with God!
Just as Christ was raised from the dead
God's power raises new life within me

I am a Child of The Living God
He is my *'Abba'* Father ~ my *'daddy'*!
I am an heir of Christ and I live in Him!

~~~

**Listen to God's heart....**
*"Live in My love, joy, peace, patience, kindness, goodness, faithfulness, gentleness, and self-control" (Gal 5:22-23)*

## PRAYER 33
*Inspired by Romans 8:18-30*

God has a wonderful future for me!
All creation longs to see God's children
And the hope that we share in Him

For I am God's child, filled with His Spirit
He helps me pray for the good of all
He helps me declare God's glory to the nations

As I speak His Word in prayer, by His Spirit
God works all things together for good
And I become more like Jesus day by day

**Listen to God's heart....**
*"The earth will be filled with My Glory; and you are being transformed to be like My Son" (Hab 2:14 / 2 Cor 3:18)*

## PRAYER 34
*Inspired by Romans 8:31-39*

God is for me not against me!
He gave His very own Son so that
I can have victory in all things, through Him

Nothing can ever separate me from Jesus
Nothing in heaven or on earth
Nor any evil, can keep me from Him

God declared His perfect love for me
When He sent His Son; therefore I am secure
No-thing and no-one can separate me from Him!

**Listen to God's heart....**
*"I have blessed you richly; you live in My mercy, peace and love, and I hold you securely in Jesus" (Jude 1)*

## PRAYER 35
*Inspired by Galatians 5:1-5*

I am set free by Jesus!
I am no longer under religious law
I live in God's grace and mercy!

My faith in Christ pleases God
My righteousness comes from Him alone
I do not try to earn His love, it is mine!

He loves me, freely from His grace
He freely gives me His righteousness
And I declare my love by trusting in Him

~~~

**Listen to God's heart....**
*"Listen up! I have forgiven you! I AM not counting sins!
Trust Me and let Me love you" (2 Cor 5:19 / John 3:16)*

## PRAYER 36
*Inspired by Ephesians 1:1-10*

I am blessed with every spiritual blessing
Through Christ, in heavenly places!
I have been adopted into God's Family!

He chose me before He created the world
Jesus made me 'right before God'
To the delight of The Father's Heart!

The glorious wisdom of God is Christ Himself
All things in heaven or on earth, one day,
Will come together under Him!

**Listen to God's heart....**
*"Jesus is alive in you, to give you a glorious hope and power within you to do good" (Eph 1:18-20 / Luke 17:21)*

## PRAYER 37
*Inspired by Ephesians 6:10-18*

I am strong in The Lord and
I am filled with His mighty power!
I am covered with the full armour of God!

I can stand fast against the devil and all his lies
With the belt of truth wrapped around me
And I can walk in the peace that comes from God

I can hold up my shield of faith to keep me strong
And protect My mind with the hope of His salvation
My spiritual sword is His Word and prayer!

~~~

**Listen to God's heart....**
*"In Christ you can do all things; even if you feel weak, I give you My grace to enable you" (Phil 4:13 / 2 Cor 12:9)*

## PRAYER 38
*Inspired by Colossians 1:15-23*

The invisible God is seen in Jesus!
Through Him, God made everything that exists
And He holds all things together by His Word

The fullness of God lives in Jesus!
Through Him, God reconciled everything to Himself
And this includes me ~ I am reconciled to God!

I can now stand before His Presence without fault
All because of Jesus ~ so I stand in this truth and
Proclaim this Good News to the whole world!

~~~

**Listen to God's heart....**
*"I sent Jesus to share the Good News that I love you and want you to know Me as I really am" (John 1:18+3:16-17)*

## PRAYER 39
*Inspired by Jude 1-2 / 20-25*

I am dearly loved by God The Father
And kept secure by Jesus Christ!
He fills my heart with mercy, peace and love!

I build myself up in faith by looking to Him
I pray in The Spirit and in the Love of God
And I cast off all doubt and worry

For He is able to keep me from falling
So I can stand before God without shame
All the honour goes to Jesus and all that He is!

**Listen to God's heart....**
*"I watch over you and keep you steady in your walk with Me; so do not fear, trust in Me" (Ps 121:3 / John 14:1)*

## PRAYER 40
*Inspired by Revelation 1:10-18*

Lord Jesus, Your voice is magnificent
Like the sound of a trumpet blast!
And Your Face shines like the sun!

Your Voice is like mighty rushing water
A refreshing delight to my soul
And Your Eyes are like blazing fire!

You are too awesome to behold
Yet You tell me not to fear and place
Your Hand of blessing upon my head!

~~~

**Listen to God's heart....**
*"I AM The Alpha and Omega, The Beginning and The End
~ you are alive in Me and you are blessed! (Rev 22:13-14)*

# PRAYERS OF PRAISE AND THANKSGIVING

## PRAYER 41
*Inspired by Psalm 19:1-8*

Thank You Lord for each new morning
All creation praises You day and night
In silence, yet in awe and wonder

I thank You for the rising of the sun
Then when it sets, for the moon and stars
That shine throughout the night

I praise You for being worthy of my trust
Thank You for being faithful to me
For Your strength and wisdom every day

~~~

**Listen to God's heart....**
*"I AM your Rock of Strength and I have chosen you to share in the life of My Son" (Deut 32:4 /1 Cor 1:9)*

## PRAYER 42
*Inspired by Psalm 145:1-8*

I praise You my Lord and King!
I bless Your Name forever
And I delight to sing Your praise!

For You are great and glorious
Each generation will worship You
And sing of Your awesome deeds

When I think of Your Majesty, I am thankful!
For You are kind and compassionate
Slow to anger and rich in love!

~~~

**Listen to God's heart....**
*"I AM filled with compassion for you ~ I AM not angry,
I AM gracious and merciful to you always" (Is 30:18)*

# PRAYER 43
## *Inspired by Isaiah 35:1-10*

Thank You Lord for Your life giving water
In Your Love You pour water in the desert
And cause wastelands to blossom

Thank You for the courage You give me
When I am fearful, You make me bold
When I am weak You make me strong

Thank You for preparing a path for me
Where I can walk in safety
And for crowning my head with joy!

~~~

**Listen to God's heart....**
*"I make a way where there seems no way; I turn mourning into dancing, and sorrow into joy" (Is 43:16 / Ps 30:11)*

## PRAYER 44
*Inspired by Isaiah 42:5-17*

Thank You for giving me life
And for placing Your Hand in mine
So that I may rejoice in new things!

Lord I will sing a new song to You!
A song of praise and thankfulness
To give glory and honour to You!

Thank You for turning darkness into light
And for making rough places smooth
And leading me along a fresh path!

~~~

**Listen to God's heart....**
*"In Me is newness of life; you are a new creation and you have a new song to sing!" (Rom 6:4 / 2 Cor 5:17 / Ps 98:1)*

## PRAYER 45
*Inspired by John 20:19-31*

Thank You Father that Jesus has risen!
I praise You that He is alive!
And thank You for the peace that He gives

Thank You for the gift of Your Holy Spirit
And that Jesus has paid for all my sin
Thank You that I am forgiven!

Thank You for all Your blessings
Which You freely give as I trust in Your Son
Thank You for Your grace, mercy, and love.

~~~

**Listen to God's heart....**
*"Jesus has risen from the dead just as He promised; He is with you and is praying for you" (Matt 28:5-6 / Heb 7:25)*

## PRAYER 46
### *Inspired by Romans 5:1-11*

I praise You glorious Father
How incredible are Your ways
In Christ I have peace with Holy God!

Thank You for the eternal hope that You give
And the love You have poured into my heart!
Christ showed Your great love for me at The Cross!

Thank You that I am Your friend
I will boast only of the goodness of God
And praise You with my whole heart

~~~

**Listen to God's heart....**
*"I have chosen you and call you My friend ~ be at peace, for I AM at peace with you" (John 15:15 / 2 John 1:3)*

## PRAYER 47
*Inspired by Philippians 2:5-11*

Thank You Jesus for Your gracious heart!
Although The Lord of all creation, You chose to
Become a man and live as one of us upon the earth!

Thank You for Your willingness
To give Your life at The Cross, in order to
Save all mankind from sin and eternal death

No wonder God has exalted Your Great Name!
One day every name will bow at Your feet
To the glory of God The Father!

~~~

**Listen to God's heart....**
*"One day, everyone will know and recognise My Son; so continue to live and grow in Him" (Phil 2:11 / Col 2:6-7)*

## PRAYER 48
*Inspired by 1 Peter 1:3-9*

I praise You Father God for Your mercy
And Your grace displayed in Jesus for all to see!
Thank You for the 'new life' I have in Him!

I praise You for my inheritance in Christ
The great and living hope to which I am called
That is kept safe in Heaven for me!

Although I do not see Jesus with my natural eyes
I know Him and love Him, and I believe in Him
For He is the joy and salvation of my soul!

**Listen to God's heart....**
*"You are saved by My grace and by your faith in Jesus; you also share in His inheritance" (Eph 2:8 / Rom 8:17)*

## PRAYER 49
*Inspired by 1 John 3:1-3 / 19-24*

Thank You for lavishing Your love on me!
How wonderful to be called Your child
And to become more like Your Son!

Thank You that my heart can be at peace
For You do not condemn me
Therefore, I will not condemn myself!

Thank You for the love of Jesus
I praise You that He enables me
To love others by His Sprit, as He loves me!

~~~

**Listen to God's heart....**
*"My command to love is not difficult, because I live in you; just let Me love through you" (John 13:34-35 / 1 John 5:3)*

## PRAYER 50
*Inspired by Revelation 22:1-17*

Thank You Lord for Your life giving water!
Thank You for Your Tree of Life
That can heal nations!

I praise You for the brightness of Your glory
That will one day light up all creation
For You reign over heaven and earth!

You are The Bright Morning Star
Who gives light to all who come to You!
Thank You for free gift of eternal life!

~~~

**Listen to God's heart....**
*"I give living water to all who ask of Me; I AM The Tree of Life; to know Me is to know eternal life" (John 7:38+17:3)*

## Your inheritance in Christ

As co-heirs with Christ (Rom 8:17), you and I share an eternal and glorious inheritance with Him (Col 3:24 / Heb 9:15 / 1 Peter 1:4). To encourage, here are some examples of what this means:

- You are a new creation (2 Cor 5:17)
- You are born of imperishable seed (1 Peter 1:23)
- You are part of God's Family (Heb 2:11)
- You are His dearly loved child (1 John 3:1)
- You are part of Christ's Body (Rom 12:5)
- You are part of God's Field / His Building (1 Cor 3:9)
- You are sealed by His Holy Spirit (2 Cor 1:22)
- You are guarded by God Himself (John 17:11)
- No one can take you from Him (John 10:28-29)
- No one can take His love away (Rom 8:39)
- God Himself will wipe away your tears (Rev 21:4)
- You have eternal life (John 3:16)
- You have eternal hope (Eph 1:18)
- You have treasure in heaven (Matt 6:19-20 )

# BLESSINGS

*A selection of personalised/paraphrased
Bible readings to offer help in times of need*

## *What does The Bible say about loneliness and isolation?*

*In Genesis 28:15 God says ~ He goes with you wherever you go, so you are never truly alone*

*In Exodus 33:14 God says ~ His presence is with you*

*In Isaiah 41:10 God promises ~ that He will help and strengthen you, and always be with you*

*In Isaiah 43:2 God says ~ when situations arise that seem overwhelming, He will not leave you*

*In Isaiah 49:16 God says ~ your name is written on His hands and you are always in His thoughts*

*Psalm 42:8 says ~ that God's love is with you by day and His song is with you at night, like a prayer*

*Psalm 46:7 says ~ God is with you all the time*

*In Matthew 28:20 Jesus said ~ He is and will always be with you*

*In John 14:16-18 Jesus said ~ that The Holy Spirit would also live inside you as a believer*

*In John 14:23 + John 16:27 Jesus said ~ God The Father loves you and delights to make His home in you*

*In Hebrews 13:5 God says ~ He will never, NEVER leave you nor forsake you*

*Romans 8:39 + Romans 12:5 say ~ nothing can separate you from God's love and that all believers in Jesus belong to 'Christ's Body'*

*Colossians 1:27 + Galatians 2:20 say ~ Jesus Himself lives in you, as a believer in His Name*

**Therefore, you are never alone ~ God is with you**

Reader's personal notes

## What does The Bible say about fear and anxiety?

*Psalm 46:1 says ~ God is your refuge and strength; and He is always there to help you in times of trouble*

*Psalm 56:3-4 says ~ it is good to praise God and to trust His Word when you are anxious or fearful*

*In Isaiah 35:4 God says ~ "I AM the God who rescues you, so do not fear"*

*In Isaiah 41:10 God says ~ "Do not be disheartened for I AM with you to strengthen and help you. I will uphold you with My very own powerful right hand!"*

*In Zephaniah 3:17 God says ~ He loves you and is with you; He is your Saviour, who delights and sings over you!*

*In Matthew 14:27 Jesus said ~ "Take heart and do not be afraid!"*

*In Luke 10:19 Jesus said ~ "I have given you spiritual authority so do not fear, you have the power to overcome"*

*In John 14:1 Jesus said ~ "Do not allow your heart to be troubled or upset, trust in God, trust in Me!*

*In John 16:33 Jesus said ~ "Find peace in Me. In this world there are many troubles BUT I have overcome the world! Have confidence in Me"*

*Philippians 4:5-7 says ~ do not look around you anxiously but instead pray about everything. Look to Jesus; for His peace will guard your heart and mind*

*1 Peter 5:7 says ~ to cast all your anxiety on Him for He cares for you, all the time!*

*1 John 5:4-5 says ~ everyone born of God overcomes! And through faith in Christ you are God's beloved child!*

**Therefore, take heart, you overcome in Him!**

## Reader's personal notes

..................................................................................

..................................................................................

..................................................................................

..................................................................................

..................................................................................

..................................................................................

..................................................................................

..................................................................................

..................................................................................

..................................................................................

..................................................................................

## *What does The Bible say about depression and sadness?*

*Psalm 3:3 says ~ God is like a shield around you and He lifts up your head*

*Psalm 9:9 says ~ God is your shelter and protection*

*Psalm 23:4 says ~ God comforts you even when you feel like you are walking through a deep valley*

*Psalm 30:11 says ~ God will turn your mourning into dancing, and your sadness into joy*

*Psalm 34:17-18 says ~ that God hears you; and when you are brokenhearted, He rescues you; and when you are feeling crushed, He restores you*

*Isaiah 26:3 says ~ keeping your thoughts on God, it will help your heart to find peace*

*Nehemiah 8:10 says ~ the joy of The Lord is your strength*

*Isaiah 40:31 says ~ when you look to the Lord and hope in Him, you will begin to renew your strength; and you will rise up like an eagle!*

*Isaiah 60:1 says ~ that God's Light and Glory shines upon you! He will help you learn to overcome depression and enjoy newness of life; for in Him you radiate His Light!*

*In Matthew 11:28-30 Jesus said ~ "Come to Me when you are weary, I will give you rest and peace to lift your heart. Let Me carry your burden and refresh your soul"*

*In John 10:28-29 Jesus said ~ that no one can snatch you out of His hand!*

*Romans 8:31+38-39 says ~ God is for you not against you and nothing can separate you from His love*

*Hebrews 13:6 says ~ The Lord is your helper at all times*

**God is compassionate; He comforts you with His love, helps you and watches over you**

## Reader's personal notes

..............................................................................
..............................................................................
..............................................................................
..............................................................................
..............................................................................
..............................................................................
..............................................................................
..............................................................................
..............................................................................
..............................................................................
..............................................................................
..............................................................................

### What does The Bible say about guidance and purpose?

*Psalm 32:8 says ~ God will instruct you, teach you and council you in ways that are best for you; and He promises to always watch over you*

*Psalm 119:105 + 138:8 says ~ God's Word is a light to your path and that God will fulfil His purpose in you*

*Proverbs 3:5-6 says ~ to trust in The Lord with all your heart and do not only rely on your own thinking. As you put Him first, He will straighten out the road before you*

*Isaiah 30:21 + 58:11 say ~ God will speak to you to guide you and that He delights to guide you*

*Jeremiah 29:11 says ~ He always has GOOD plans for you, and that He gives you hope and a future*

*Luke 1:79 says ~ that God shines light into your path to help guide you forward*

*John 14:26 says ~ The Holy Spirit will teach you and guide you; and He will help you remember what Jesus has said*

*John 16:13 says ~ The Holy Spirit will only speak truth to you and will reveal the Father's will for you*

*Romans 12:1-2 says ~ to retrain your thinking so that you think as God thinks according to His Word. This will help your life to be a spiritual sacrifice that pleases God; and you will be able to discern His will clearer as you do this*

*Ephesians 2:10 says ~ that you are God's work of art! You were created for good works that He has prepared for you*

*Hebrews 13:21 says ~ He will equip you with good things to do His will*

*James 1:5-6 says ~ if you need wisdom simply ask of God who delights to give to you. But do not doubt, for He loves to do you good*

**God delights to lead and guide you; He can be trusted**

## Reader's personal notes

..................................................................
..................................................................
..................................................................
..................................................................
..................................................................
..................................................................
..................................................................
..................................................................
..................................................................
..................................................................
..................................................................
..................................................................

## What does The Bible say about peace and reconciliation?

*Psalm 29:11 says ~ God gives strength and peace*

*Isaiah 9:6 says ~ Jesus is The Prince of Peace*

*Isaiah 26:3 says ~ that keeping your mind on Him will help your heart be at peace*

*Isaiah 54:10 says ~ God has made a covenant of peace with you, which can never be shaken nor removed*

*In John 14:27 Jesus said ~ "I give you My peace, which is greater than the world"*

*In John 16:33 Jesus said ~ that He has overcome the world so you can be at peace in your heart*

*Romans 5:1 says ~ by faith we have peace with God*

*Romans 8:6 says ~ that to set your mind on The Spirit is life and peace for you*

*Romans 12:18 says ~ that wherever possible, to live at peace with others*

*2 Corinthians 5:17-21 says ~ God has made you a new creation and given you the ministry of reconciliation*

*Colossians 1:20 says ~ God has reconciled you to Himself through Jesus at The Cross*

*Colossians 3:16 says ~ let Christ's peace rule in your heart*

*Ephesians 2:14 says ~ Jesus provides reconciliation, from God to man, and for man to man*

*Philippians 4:7 says ~ the peace of God will guard your heart and mind*

*Galations 5:22 says ~ that peace is a fruit of The Spirit*

*Philemon 1:3 says ~ God gives you grace and peace*

**Jesus is your peace and He has reconciled you to God**

## Reader's personal notes

................................................................
................................................................
................................................................
................................................................
................................................................
................................................................
................................................................
................................................................
................................................................
................................................................
................................................................
................................................................

### What does The Bible say about forgiveness and guilt?

*Psalm 103:10-14 says ~ that God does not deal with you according to your sins but He removes sin far from you, because He loves you and has great compassion on you*

*Isaiah 1:18+53:5 say ~ God Himself washes you clean, for Jesus paid for all sin*

*Isaiah 6:7 says ~ God has taken your guilt away*

*Daniel 9:9 says ~ that although everyone has rebelled against God in some way, He is merciful and forgiving*

*Zechariah 7:9 says ~ God desires for people to be honest, and show kindness and forgiveness to each other*

*In Luke 23:34 Jesus prayed ~ "Father forgive them, they do not know what they are doing"*

*John 3:16-17 says ~ God sent Jesus into this world to save you not to condemn you*

*Romans 3:22-24 says ~ God declares all who trust in Jesus to be 'not guilty'... because He takes take away your sin*

*Romans 8:1-2 says ~ that God does not condemn you, because Jesus has set you free from sin*

*2 Corinthians 7:10 says ~ that godly sorrow leads to true repentance, which God honours and He saves you*

*Ephesians 2:8 says ~ that God's forgiveness is a free gift*

*1 Timothy 2:4 says ~ God desires for all people to know Him and be saved*

*1 John 1:9 says ~ that when we are honest with God, He cleanses us from all sin*

*1 John 2:2 says ~ that Jesus has provided payment for sin for the whole world (as a gift to simply receive!)*

**Your trust in Christ frees you from all shame and guilt**

## Reader's personal notes

## *What does The Bible say about failure and doubt?*

*Deuteronomy 31:8 says ~ that no matter what happens, God remains with you*

*Proverbs 24:16 says ~ if you fall, you shall rise up again!*

*Proverbs 26:11 says ~ it is best for your life that you don't return to something that has been bad for you*

*Psalm 37:23-24 says ~ God holds your hand and He will uphold you even when you stumble*

*Psalm 40:2-3 says ~ that God lifts you up and gives you a new song to sing!*

*Psalm 145:14 says ~ God raises you up when you feel low*

*Lamentations 3:22-23 says ~ His mercies are new each morning, so any trouble or failure will not consume you*

*Isaiah 41:9 says ~ that God has never rejected you*

*Isaiah 43:18 says* ~ *to forget failures of the past but instead look to the new thing God is doing in your life*

*In Mark 11:23 Jesus said* ~ *"Do not doubt, have faith ...for whatever you speak out in faith will be done for you!"*

*2 Corinthians 4:9 says* ~ *that trouble and failure will not destroy you, for God is with you*

*Philippians 3:13-14 says* ~ *to press on forward in life.... keep looking to Jesus and follow Him*

*Philippians 4:13 says* ~ *Jesus is your strength and He gives you the ability to succeed*

*2 Timothy 1:7 says* ~ *God's Spirit has given you power, self-discipline and a sound mind to carry on!*

*James 1:6 + Romans 15:13 say* ~ *doubts cause pain and indecision but trusting God will fill you with joy and hope!*

**Rise up with faith in your heart; God never rejects you! He is patient with you and will lead you forward in life**

## Reader's personal notes

### What does The Bible say about the truth of God's Word?

*Proverbs 4:20-22 says ~ God's Words are life and healing*

*Proverbs 30:5 says ~ every word that God speaks is perfect and true, and is a shield for those who trust Him*

*Psalm 119:105 says ~ His Word is a lamp that shines to light your path*

*Isaiah 40:8 says ~ that His Word will last forever*

*Isaiah 55:10-11 says ~ God's Word will always achieve what He sent it to do*

*In Matthew 4:4 Jesus said ~ people need both spiritual and physical food; the Word of God is our spiritual food*

*Luke 8:11 says ~ God's Word is like a 'seed' (e.g. when planted in your heart...it grows to do good for you)*

*John 1:1+14 say ~ that Jesus is The Living Word of God*

*In John 5:39 Jesus said ~ the Scriptures were written to point mankind to Him and the eternal life He freely gives*

*In John 6:63 Jesus said ~ His Words are spirit and life*

*In John 17:17 Jesus said ~ that God's Word is Truth*

*Romans 15:4 says ~ the written Word of God was given to teach, encourage and give hope*

*Ephesians 6:17 says ~ The Sword of The Spirit is The Word of God*

*2 Timothy 3:16-17 says ~ all Scripture is 'God-breathed' and that He teaches and trains you through what it says*

*Hebrews 4:12 says ~ God's Word is alive and powerful!*

*Hebrews 10:16 says ~ His Word is written on your heart*

*1 Peter 1: 25 says ~ The Word of God is Good News!*

**God teaches through His Word, not by giving bad things; He is good, His Word is true, and He gives good gifts to you!** *(See: Psalm 136:1 / Psalm 18:30 / James 1:17-18)*

## Reader's personal notes

*The Lord loves to bless you*

*He delights to watch over you*

*And shine His face upon you*

*And to give you His peace*

From Numbers 26:24-26

### *Encouragement from God's Son*

I AM the way, and the truth, and the life. Come to the Father through The Son. I came to show you what the Father is really like, for I came from the very heart of God to call you to be His child forever. No darkness can ever extinguish My Light, for it is eternal and ever-living. As God's very own child, My Light lives in you.

So let your light shine for all to see, which honours your Father in Heaven, who loves you all the time, yesterday, today and forever! I AM The Bridge of eternal life, I do not condemn, I offer forgiveness and love. Trust in Me with all your heart, and I will show you the way.

*Related Scriptures: John 14:6*
*John 1:12-18 / John 1:5 / Matt 5:16*
*Col 1:27 / Heb 13:8 / 1 John 3:1*
*John 3:16-17 / Matt 11:28 / Prov 3:5-6*

## ABOUT THE AUTHOR AND GARDENLAND

John and Carmel Carberry became Christians in 1982, and were married in 1983.

Over the years they have served in church and community life, leading to the development of Gardenland Ministries (inspired by the Bible verse Isaiah 58:11).

'Gardenland' began as a group of family and friends meeting together to study the Charis Bible College Correspondence Course, while they lived in Bedford (UK).

Their family and fellowship felt the Holy Spirit's lead for Carmel to begin writing books of encouragement, sharing things God had shown the family over the years.

In 2018, John and Carmel moved to North Derbyshire to live and serve in the church and community there. They continue to offer books online at Amazon across the world.

Also available are social media and websites with free resources in the same theme of bringing hope to people anywhere, whoever they are. May you be blessed as you learn more about God's Eternal Love for you personally.

> *Isaiah 58:11*
> *The Lord will guide you continually, giving you water when you are dry and restoring your strength ~ you will be a well-watered garden, like an ever flowing spring*

---

### * YOU MATTER TO GOD *

---

# BOOKS SHARING GOOD NEWS
## *By Carmel Carberry*

**The His Story Book Series** (simple Bible book overviews)

- HIS STORY (Volume 1) ~ GENESIS
- HIS STORY (Volume 2) ~ THE GOSPELS
- HIS STORY (Volume 3) ~ ACTS and The New Testament Letters
- HIS STORY (Volume 4) *coming soon*

~~~~~

**Gardenland Books**

(personal testimony / prophetic words / looking to The Son)

- GOD'S FRUITFUL GARDEN
  *A book of Hope and Encouragement*
- COMMUNION WITH GOD *Soaring on Eagles Wings*
- SONRISE *Heaven Scent*
- SONSET *On The Throne*
- SONDOWN *A Taste of Heaven on Earth* (inc. Bible Studies)
- PROMISES *Messages from God's Heart to yours*

- **PRAYERS AND BLESSINGS** *Help in Times of Need*
- **CONTRAST**
  *looks at Bible Covenants and the 'NEW YOU' in Christ*
- **OUR IDENTITY IN CHRIST**
  *looks further at who we are in Him*
- **ANY YEAR DIARY**
  *with colour pictures and Bible verses for each week*
- **ENCOURAGEMENT NOTEBOOK**
  *a notetaking journal with messages of hope*

~~~~

**The Abi Tails Books Series** *(just for fun!)*

Funny stories about the family dog 'ABI' looking at life from a dog's point of view! With puppy pictures in full colour ~ suitable for all ages.

- ABI TAILS Volume 1 ~ *Training my humans*
- ABI TAILS Volume 2 ~ *New Adventures*

## WEBSITES & SOCIA MEDIA LINKS

MINISTRY WEBSITE: www.gardenlandministries.uk

AUTHORS BLOG: https://carmelcarberry.wordpress.com/

EMAIL gardenlandministries@gmail.com

FACEBOOK:

www.facebook.com/CarmelCarberry - Author

www.facebook.com/groups/gardenlandministries

TWITTER AND INSTAGRAM:

https://twitter.com/CarmelCarberry

https://www.instagram.com/carmelcarberry/

## A MESSAGE FROM GOD'S HEART

I love you so much that I sent My one and only Son, so that through faith in Him you can receive eternal life. I did not send Him to condemn or punish you, I sent Him to rescue you. All people everywhere have sinned, but I have demonstrated My Love for all people by sending Jesus to die on The Cross to pay for sin forever.

By faith, you can receive My free gift of salvation, for I have already provided it for you, freely by My Grace, and now you simply receive it by putting your trust in Jesus.

When you receive My Son into your heart, a spiritual new birth happens within you ~ you become My Dearly Beloved Child forever, and you become a New Creation!

As you continue to look to My Son day by day, My Holy Spirit will teach and guide you, and I will rejoice over you with singing!

*With Eternal Love & Blessing*
*From your Heavenly Father*

*Related Bible verses: John 3:16-17 / Rom 3:22-24+5:8 / Eph 2:8 / John 1:12 / 2 Cor 5:17 / John 16:13 / Zeph 3:17*

*Please say this prayer from your heart if you would like to make Jesus Lord and Saviour of your life.....*

## PRAYER

Dear Lord Jesus, Thank You that You have always loved me. I admit that I have lived my life for myself. I am sorry and repent of my sin.

Thank You that You died on The Cross to save me. I receive the forgiveness that You earned for me. I believe that You rose from the dead and are now seated at the right hand of The Father.

Please come into my heart to be my Lord and Saviour. Thank You that the moment I asked, You came in, to be with me forever! Please fill me with Your Holy Spirit and empower me with good gifts to help others. To the honour of Your Name. Amen

### *Welcome to God's Family!*
*John 1:12 (from the Amplified Bible)*
*All who receive and welcome Him ~ He gives the right to become children of God, that is, to those who believe in*
*(trust in and rely on) His Name.*

## When you trust in Jesus, The Bible says these things about you....

...you are a new creation (2 Cor 5:17) you are blessed (Eph 1:3) you are God's child (John 1:12) you are redeemed (Eph 1:7-8) you are included in God's eternal plan (Eph 1:13)

...you have His strength and power living within you (Eph 1:19-21) you are alive in Christ and filled with God's love (Eph 2:4-6) you are seated in Heavenly places with Jesus, spiritually (Eph 2:6) you are 'hand-made' by God, His work of art (Eph 2:10)

...you have eternal access to God, without fear or shame (Eph 2:17-18) you are part of God's living temple, where He delights to live (Eph 2:21-22) you share in the promises of Christ as one of His heirs (Eph 3:6)

...you can approach God with freedom and confidence (Eph 3:12) you are being strengthened by Him in your inner being (Eph 3:16) you are loved much more than you can mentally comprehend (Eph 3:18-19)

...you have His power at work in you to do more than you can imagine (Eph 3:20) you are being built up and equipped for service (Eph 4:11-13)

...you have favour with God but He has no favourites, all are loved equally (Eph 6:9) you are strong in The Lord and His mighty power (Eph 6:10) you overcome spiritual darkness though His Light and His Word (Eph 6:12-13)

...you have His truth, righteousness, peace, faith, salvation, Spirit and Word to enable you (Eph 6:14-17) you have the love and peace of Christ within you, forever and for all time (Eph 6:23)

*Enjoy these truths and enjoy your new relationship with God! Please use the resources and links mentioned on the previous pages to encourage and bless your journey with Him*

Printed in Great Britain
by Amazon